UnLocked

Published by Accent Press Ltd – 2009
ISBN 9781907016400

Printed and bound in the UK

Cover design by James Ford Design
www.jfd.co.uk

Poetry is not a form of expression readily associated with young people in custody. Yet I know from my visits to secure establishments in England and Wales how poetry can resonate with young people serving custodial sentences. Books of poetry are often as popular with young people in custody as stories by the best known crime or thriller writers.

Young people in the juvenile secure estate in England and Wales have been encouraged to submit their own work for inclusion in this collection. It represents an extraordinary expression of the regrets, fears and dreams of a group of young people whose voices are rarely heard. Many of the poems reflect on the circumstances that have led the writer to custody, and express feelings of pain or sorrow that may not have been articulated before.

I hope that you enjoy the poems within this collection and that reading them provides a brief insight into the experiences, talent and imagination of the young people whose work is represented here.

Frances Done,
Chair, Youth Justice Board
November 2009

Our thanks go to Nathan Ward, Enrichment Manager at Medway Secure Training Centre, for the inspiration that led to this project getting off the ground, for sifting the many entries we received and having the difficult task of choosing what to include.

We would also like to thank the young people who have taken the time to submit their entries and hope that they enjoy reading the book as much as we have enjoyed putting it together.

G4S Care & Justice Services

Once I was here, then I was gone,
I went to Prison for something I hadn't done.

I should be at school doing my GCSE's,
Instead I'm in here getting PCC's

I miss my friends, I miss my family,
I need help, so please tell me.

I want to be normal, not well known,
I just want to be with my family at home.

Why was I there on that hot summer's day?
I wish I would have just stayed away.

I've ruined my life,
All because of a knife.

Wasted 8 months because of a mistake.
Now I think we should retake.

I lose my temper really easy,
So please don't tease me.

I see the psychologist about my fears,
And sometimes even share my tears.

When I go home, I'm going to turn my life
around,
And am going to make everyone so proud.

by Alexandra K, age 15
Rainsbrook Secure Training Centre

Since I was little
I have been in care
It's just something I could not bear

At the age of 2
My mum had gone
Then I was singing the lonely song

Sitting on the door step
Crying for my mum
My dad like what's gone on

In my mind
I'm thinking is this right
Or am not thinking bright

Going to school
Day by day
Fitting in like a piece of cake
Not saying my behaviour been great

See I am not saying
I don't need addiction
And I'm not saying
I'm not a pain in the ass
And I don't roll around in grass

But you see sometimes
People try and help me
But sometimes I punch them away
That's because people say
I love you and I care for you
Then they leave you then abuse you
And leave you on the door step
Crying your eyes
Maybe if there was someone to stay
Then life would be more like clay.

by Holly C, age 13
Medway Secure Training Centre

What I've Got

I was here but now I'm not
I'm around the corner in a yacht
I'm sailing to a nicer spot
I need some money cause £10 is all I've got
I need to feed my baby who is in a cot
In the fridge is a loaf of bread and it is starting to rot
I looked around and found a pot now £10 and penny is what I've got

by Scott C, age 14
Swanwick Lodge Secure Children's Home

Be

A musician I wish to be
Like a magician I perform tricks
So that every night next to you I will be
Sad I will never be
Because like a physician better you make me be

by Pedro A, age 16
HMP & YOI Brinsford

THINK!

Sticks and stones may break my bones
but names will never hurt me.
Pride, passion and dignity,
these things will never desert me.

We're all different races,
from different backgrounds
and different places.

Speak to us on a one
to one basis
you will find out more than
looking at our faces.

Consider how the other
person would feel.
This shouldn't be a case
of deal or no deal.

Sticks and stones may break my bones
but names will never hurt me.
Pride, passion and dignity,
these things will never desert me.

Just remember before
you mention.
You could cause upset,
pain or tension.

This would prevent
guilt and redemption
which raises the
right intention.

You need to learn
more common sense, because
when you're racist
it's an offence.

All it brings is victims
of neglect, due to
ignorance and lack of
respect.

Sticks and stones may break my bones
but names will never hurt me.
Pride, passion and dignity,
these things will never desert me.

*by Nevin R, age 17, Stephen L, age 17, Perry H,
age 17, Nathan D, age 16, and Jonathan P, age
16*
HMP & YOI Parc

Actions and consequences

Banged up locked down
Sentence riding slow
Fists clenched mind racing
Screaming let me go.
Messed up people messed up times
How did it come to this,
I bow my head and raid my thoughts
Its time to reminisce...
...they stand together all alone
Or at least they think they are,
I pull up my hood slip out my blade
And slowly approach the car.
I scream and shout and yell abuse
My mind has gone all blank
Flash of silver splash of red
Screaming there's only you to thank.
Red mist fading hands stained red
As sirens are closing in
My life's over mistakes been made
I've lived a life of sin.
I raise my head and look around
My nightmare will never end,
I'm forced to stay behind these bars
With my memories as my only friend.

by Hollie D, age 15
Hassockfield Secure Training Centre

Hello World,
Everything beautiful,
Long have I been locked in this pit,
Late I have stayed until I'm lullabyed,
Only I have high walls round me.

Found dead in a muddy ditch,
Laying with his head gone,
Alone waiting to be buried,
Starved of a place to sleep,
Hating the gun that flashed.

For hours I wait, days upon time,
Under the circumstances I don't want to talk,
Can I break free from this cold cell,
Killed by boredom in this white room.

Tapes record every word I utter
Hate is the word that I mutter,
Every second I'm hating this.

Police got me waiting in here
On the way down I was saying "shit"
Living like a crook with an itchy blanket
I've been here, done that,
Can't I ever get free
Every day I get arrested.

by Benjamin B, age 15
Medway Secure Training Centre

Go to Jail

That's me in Jail
My face looks pale
Sitting down in my pad
Feeling sad
Why do I do
A stupid crime
And get 6 years
Every time?

Growing up in a jail
Thinking my life
Will never fail
Looking up to my big brother
Following his foot steps
Without a mother
I need help
I shouted out
But no one was there to help me

Living on leg 3
In Wetherby
Enjoing my life
As it walks by me
I have not noticed
My life is ruined
In and out I go
Prison is my home for now
All I say for all you out there
Don't make your self into a monster

We are all good and polite
We are all criminals at night
If we fight with ourselves
We might win
Change your self
Prison is no life for anyone
Any age in for any crime
Make a change live with your real family
Not the prison staff
We are all locked up
People are so sad
Family and friends are crying
Help them by not being a criminal

by Damien H, age 15
HMYOI Wetherby

Snow White

Grumpy was all short and small
He never smiled or laughed at all

Dopey was a bit of a joker
He lost the lot in a game of poker

Sneezy always sneezed a lot
Such that he began to lose the plot

Bashful was meek and shy
He never looked you in the eye

Happy was tall and thin
He also had a big fat grin

Sleepy was always on his back
You could never get him out of his sack

Snow White was the fairest of them all
It drove her stepmother up the wall

Her stepmother was evil and rude
So she decided to poison the food

Snow White fell fast asleep
The handsome prince began to weep

He kissed her on her lips so red
And when she awoke they were wed

by Ann B, age 17
Oakhill Secure Training Centre

Something Special

As I wonder the clouds go by
I look up into the darkening skies.
And pin all my thoughts and dreams on a place
That's not as bad as it seems.
The sun that shines upon my face,
Helps me to find my place
The rays of hope that shines on me
Makes me feel wild and free
I long to be happy and my life true
This wish will be mine,
Since I got you
Watch out for my night and day
I am so lucky you came my way.

by Najwa H, age 17
HMP &YOI Eastwood Park

The view from the Hood

I am a young man with feelings
Who didn't quite know
The meaning of people looking at me
Like the alarm bells were ringing.
Putting away their mobile phones
when they see me coming.

What I see is not what they see.
I see a young, smart, black boy with potential,
but they see a black boy in a hood,
which must make me a criminal in their eyes.

What people see and hear of others are just lies;
thinking they're gonna die
When they see my guys coming round the corner
Wearing hoodies.
Not knowing that they might be goody goodies

by Sanchez B, age 16
Rainsbrook Secure Training Centre

The Crashing Waves

When the waves crash against the shore,
And the wind is blowing hard and cold.
The clouds are looking dark and gloomy,
And the falling rain is hard and drowning.
With the cracking of thunder across the sky,
It's as if the world is going to die.
Lightening flashes so intense and fierce,
Your eyes slam shut against your tears,
Then your frozen blue lips begin to tremble,
With desperation you begin to run,
But the ground beneath you becomes disturbed,
You're giving up all hope,
You're beginning to panic,
With the tide so close and so loud,
It drowns out all other sounds,
As you hear the waves smashing off the ground.
The jagged rocks are perched at your feet,
When you violently fall and smash your head.
It seems to be that you're as good as dead.
But your fear of death is all but over,
As you open your eyes and wake up in bed.

by Paul F, age 18
HMP & YOI Castington

I feel so angry
I shouldn't be here
I hate being locked up
I love my freedom

I should be out
With my mates and family

All you can hear
Is rattling keys
Footsteps
Shouting kids

Prison is not a place
My family wants to see

by Ellie M, age 16
Hassockfield Secure Training Centre

My Life

It all started when I was 14,
A few months after my parents broke up,
No-one ever asked what's up.
Couldn't speak to anyone,
Got angry with everyone.

Got kicked out of school,
Life was getting boring,
Smoking weed from the morning.
Doing nothing every day,
Committing affray.

Just done crime,
To make money,
At the time I thought it was funny.
Never thought before I act,
Got hit by the big impact.

Didn't think or care about jail,
Was just doing my thing,
Being locked up would be a big sting.
Then a long life friend died New Years Day,
Things just turned to a serious way.

Sitting in my cell, thinking about life,
Thinking about the past and future,
As I'm looking through my winda.
Same old routine everyday,
That is just the prison way.

The food is not really nice,
It is nasty,
Just like a Cornish pasty.

You get use to it after a while,
But it's still vile.

Waiting for a court date to be sentenced,
Want to know my release date,
As I want to start a fresh new slate.
Time is going fast,
Leaving behind the past.

My prison cell is like my bedroom,
It's all nice and cosy,
The staff like looking threw the flap being nosey.
I know now to think before I act,
And not to react.

Want to stay out this time,
Get my life on track,
And never have to look back.
I want to prove to my family,
The sort of man I can be.

I want to be free from crimes,
To stay off the drugs,
And keep away from the other thugs.
Smoke a bit of weed,
But still succeed.

I need to do more with my spare time,
Start a relationship,
I'm pretty sure I know with which chick.
I want to become a painter and decorator,
And to own my own business later.

by Matt B, age 16
HMYOI Stoke Heath

Bullying

Bullies are bullies, that's what they will always be.
They'll never change, just watch and you'll see.
I met this one girl, Billy she was named.
She used to get bullied, teased and shamed.
Such a nice lass, but no-one else could see,
Everybody picked on her, everyone but me.
They'd punch her and kick her and pull her long hair.
Tell her that her mum doesn't even care.
She would cry out for help, but everyone just stared,
Everyone stood there; nobody cared.
I wanted to help. I wanted them to know,
All the pain they were causing that wasn't on show.
Finally, they left her all hurting and weak.
I went over to her and she couldn't even speak.
Another day over. Billy ran through my head;
All the thoughts and the words those other girls said.
She wasn't in school the very next day.
All those other girls had nothing to say.
The head teacher told us what we needed to know.

That poor little girl had let herself go.
Twelve years old and she took all the drugs,
Because she got bullied by wannabe thugs.
Tears ran down my face; that little girl's gone.
I should have done something, but what I did was none.
The moral of this poem is that you don't know even part
Of what lay beneath that little girl's heart

by Charlotte R, age 17
Rainsbrook Secure Training Centre

The ugly duckling

This story is about an ugly duck
That needed luck
He was born with a broken nose
To top it off, he had six toes
His brothers gave him punches
And stole his school lunches
His mum didn't like him and told him to scram
So he packed up his jam
And moved to a new dam

It was here he saw a sexy swan
And wished he could be one
As he sat all on his own
He thinks to himself, 'I need a loan'
To fix up his broken bone

Ten minutes later, again he sees the swan
He thinks, 'what more could go wrong?'
He asks her, "where do you live and where do you
come from?"

After exchanging pleasantries
She asks if he is easy to please
"I got a broken nose
And to top it off, I got six toes
I am known as an ugly duck
Whose life is in the muck"

As they sit on a log
She leans over and gives him a snog
The ugly duck
Thinks, "I'm finally in luck"

The kiss makes him grow
Magic happens and he starts to glow
In the morning when he awoke
He thought he was wearing a white coat
He was all bloat

The lady swan thought he was strong
And they were married for pretty long
He become a king
And they had loads of kids that would swim and sing

by Breadon H, age 15
Oakhill Secure Training Centre

Questions

Where do I fit into all this?
Is there a place for me in this big jigsaw puzzle?
A place just the right shape for me.

Should I change just to fit in
or do I ask the world to take me as I am?
If I change, am I 'me' any more?

How do I get to the place where I belong?
If I get there, will it have been worth it?
Will I still recognise myself?

by Malcolm M, age 16
Rainsbrook Secure Training Centre

Dream

Carl who lives in a hole is an awful tempered troll
He goes hunting looking for moles
He has a belly full of rolls
His world is full of dead souls
They are looking for him till night goes dull
He wakes up, looked around then shouted YOO
My house is full up with coal
I'm looking to be the main person in this role
So that when I get out of this dream
I may be lucky to get parole

by Carl C, age 15
Swanwick Lodge Secure Children's Home

My Details

I live with:
My mum, dad, two brothers, one sister, a dog
called Bob and my son Morgan.

I've got a son called Morgan, he is 8 months old.
His birthday is on the 28th October.
I can't wait to see him.
He is small, but really chubby.
He can say
Dad
Chocolate
And Mum.
When I go back to my cell I will stick a picture of
him in my journal, cos I love him and he looks
like me.

by Simon W, age 17
HMP & YOI Parc

Realistic thoughts

I'm better than this these people don't understand
Why the hell would I do this crime for a third of a grand?
I come in here a boy now I'm the rebirth of a man
But still, these people don't understand

My biggest regret is that I didn't stand up for my belief
Now I'm in here calling another equal the chief
And some of these people label me a deceitful beast
As a matter of fact I'm much closer to a priest

Some people in here feel they have nothing to offer
To the world, to themselves so they just cause bother
Their dreams to shoot at the keeper and I'm not talking about soccer
And there was me innocently living life as a lodger

To get by, I had to accept neglect in my life
I got closer to people that would soon back bite
At one point I moved with the protection of a
knife
But with the help of someone special I detected
the right

But it's still clear in my mind like it was just
before I came here
Locked in the penitentiary and I'm not trying to
get a name here
And because I hardly associate people call me a
phoney, a fake
All I want to do is make sure I don't get out here
too late

by Nathan S, age 17
HMP & YOI Brinsford

I don't like it here
I want to break free
Back to the street where I should be
I want to be chilling
With my own mates on my own street
Relaxing and listening to all the beats.

The bad thing happened when I was so stressed
Thinking about it makes me depressed
If I was free I could be
The person that I long to be.

Being in this place so far from home
What keeps me going
Is knowing I'm not alone
I can speak to my mum on the phone.

In here you have to stick to the rules
Always waiting for your next move
Seeing all different staff most nights
Then all of a sudden there's more in sight.

I know now what I did was wrong
And I think about it all day long
Doing the same things day after day
But I know soon it will all go away
Putting my family through all this pain
And for what? What did I what did I gain.

by Laura H, age 16
Hassockfield Secure Training Centre

Might have had a better chance
Everyday I ran so fast
Didn't know where to go
Waiting round the corner on patrol
Asked me for my name and address
You're under arrest
Sent to court with my best friend
They need my paperwork so then
Court got adjourned again.

by Kieran O'S, age 14
Medway Secure Training Centre

Whilst sat here bored in my cell
With nothing to do I press my bell
Waiting a couple of mins still no body turns up
Maybe I'll go sleep they may wake me up.
I go for my dinner
Eating the same old slop
Just thinking one day I may get to the shop
Hearing the same old noises from the lads next door
I get even more bored and clean my floor.
Now I am finished with nothing to say
I stay in my pad from day to day.

by Adam R, age 18
HMYOI Wetherby

My head is banging with fear,
My freedom is finally near,
Four months banged up,
The string was cut.

The Law had given up on me,
Said I was not suitable to be free,
I got sent to Medway STC.

Riding time in this Centre,
My behaviour didn't get any better.
Always hurling abuse.

Wanting to fight different people.
No I didn't want to lose,
But to walk away would make me vulnerable,
So I chose violence instead of being bruised.

Finally it was time to give up,
My sentence is nearly done,
So I stop causing beef,
All I want is peace.

Can't wait to get out of this STC.

by Aisha McC, age 15
Medway Secure Training Centre

The Beach Scene

The beach, a wonder to some people, a hell hole
to others.
But always look on the bright side of life, like the
sun, a glowing light
Stealthily tiptoeing across the sky from east to
west.
The clouds drifting on an invisible lilo across the
vast ocean we call the sky
Looking down onto the fairy liquid – gently waves
of late summer.
They roll at a steady pace onto the shore
accompanied by a gentle wind,
Taking a sandy layer of skin from the majestic
sand dunes.
As the rubber air-filled pleasure planets called
beach balls are packed away
A harmony of goodbyes and a crescendo of
snapping deck chairs ends the day.
Good times.

by Kyle D, age 16
HMP & YOI Castington

A community of unity

Different voices, different choices,
Shop signs written in languages I don't speak.
Warm, spicy, savoury smells.
The call to prayer, the sound of bells.

A dozen different accents.
Forms of English like, but unlike my own.
English from the Caribbean,
Asian English, English English.

All of us held together by our differences;
Our cultures, our faiths, our abilities.
Finding ways to bridge the divide.
Living together side by side.

We are the bricks, the cement that builds the
community,
Some of us are doors, some of us are windows.
We need doors for privacy and mutual respect.
We need windows for a broad outlook on life.

Some would choose more locks and bolts and
bars,
But we don't want to live in a fortress of
suspicion.
We want a community built upon sharing
and the security to show each other respect.

by Martin B, age 15
Rainsbrook Secure Training Centre

Cinderella

A beautiful girl – slim and blonde
Lived by one big dirty pond

The beautiful girl was made to clean
Made to clean and make it gleam

How she wanted to go to the ball
To dress up and dance in the hall

She cried and cried, and wept and wept
She heard a weird voice and then she leapt

A short fat lady stood there with a frown
And said quite loudly, "Er's ya gown!"

The beautiful girl shone like a light
"But you must be home befow' midnight"

The beautiful girl arrived at the ball
Arrived at the ball to dance in the hall

She poured herself a glass of wine
Got to the third and began to wobble on the line

Out of the corner of her eye
She saw prince charming who was named Kye

She staggered over and took his hand
And danced all night to the royal band

The night was coming to an end
And poor prince charming was going round the
bend

The clock ding-donged as it hit midnight
And the prince charming cried with delight

The beautiful girl lost her shoe
And she was so pissed she ran to the loo

What's the moral of this tale?
Don't get bladdered on ale

by Hannah M, age 17
Oakhill Secure Ttraining Centre

Rain, Rain, Please Stay!

When the rain pours you get soaking wet
And a depressing feeling in your mind is what you
get,
But when the rain's peaceful your problems
disappear
Listening to the sound only gentle drops you can
hear,
Then your worries vanish gone in an instant
A white fluffy cloud you can see in the distance,
You're drifting off take a relax on cloud nine
Nothing can bother you now because this is your
time.

Floating and drifting through the luscious blue sky
No worry in the world no care of how high,
Thinking and hoping this feeling will last
Well I better enjoy it before it becomes the past,
The only thing you can see is the yellow circle of
the sun
Everything else is just how it had begun,
I wriggle a bit and sink further into the cloud
No worries, no noise and no being surrounded by
a crowd.

by Rhys T, age 17
HMP & YOI Parc

The frog prince

There was once a witch full of envy
She put a curse on a prince named Henry
The only way to end this spell
Was to kiss the princess Annabel
The prince was scared there was no hope
So he started smoking dope
But all the drugs done was turn him crazy
And he kept dreaming of this beautiful lady

One day it happened, his dreams came true
But he was shocked, he didn't know what to do
So he spoke out loud and screamed, "yo sexy"
And she thought to herself, "A frogs trying to
molest me"

by Abdullah A, age 14
Oakhill Secure Training Centre

August

August is the best time of the year
Understanding and remembering past times
Going out and having fun
Under the Summer sun
Sadly Summer comes to an end
Times goes by then we start again….

Jolly
Over the moon
Delightful
Inviting
Easy Going

by Jodie R, age 15
Swanwick Lodge Secure Children's Home

In here, lonely, on my own
No family, no friends, no nowt.
I wanna get my head down
So I can change and get out.

I wish I never committed a crime
Then I wouldn't be here doing my time.

In eighty one days
I'll be going home
I'm gonna keep my head down
And go it alone.

I wish I never committed a crime
Then I wouldn't be here doing my time.

My best friend was there for me
But then she weren't
So from now on
I hope that I've learnt.

I wish I never committed a crime
Then I wouldn't be here doing my time.

So here I am
In Hassockfield secure
Can't wait for the day
To be walking out of the door
I wish I never committed a crime
Then I wouldn't be here doing my time.

My mind is set
To go for my goal
That part of me missing
Should fill up the hole.

I wish I never committed a crime
Then I wouldn't be here doing my time.

by Naomi C, age 14
Hassockfield Secure Training Centre

Time

Time is life
Just passing by
Time is why
Some people cry

Time is just meaningless space
Time exists only in the human race

Time is why we are behind bars
Which is the effect
Of stealing cars

by Gervase W, age 17
HMP & YOI Parc

Caught by the police on a hot summers day,
Remanded in custody, I sit here and pray,
On the Friday I was expected in court,
YJB sat down and thought.
Down to my crime I was sentenced to life,
Oh, never again will I carry a knife,
Now all it's done is caused nothing but strife.

by Cullum M, age 13
Medway Secure Training Centre

I sit in my cell
Wondering when
My time inside will end

The judge sentenced me
To four months of hell
I am in hell

My life it has fell
My Mum shouts
Ears ring like a bell

Family and People
Must think I want to die
All for the sake of one more lie

In a suit and a tie
The judge looks me right in the eye
All they say is goodbye

People think they are thugs
To me they are just mugs
All for taking drugs

It's dinner time
They want to know my crime
My mind tricks like a dime

Clock ticks by to pass the time
Say hold it down one last time

Four months of hell

by Jordan McK, age 16
Hassockfield Secure Training Centre

My oh my, what have I done,
Eating bad food all the time.
Doing things which I do not want to do,
Waking up to a knock on the door.
Angry, but nowhere to run,
YOT are so happy I am here,
It seem like they have won.

See what this path has done to me,
Running from police,
But you eventually get caught.
Itching and scratching,
With no fresh air.
Morning after morning doing the same thing,
Eventually they turn the key and lock me away.

by Theo S, age 13
Medway Secure Training Centre

47

Holidays

I look out at the glorious view
Of pastureland and woodland scenes
And praise the Lord for His great gift
Set in a sea for various greens
Folk talk of places where they've been in foreign
countries
So exciting, where sun and sea, waves and palms
combine to make them so inviting
But I don't need to pack my bags or travel miles
to catch a plane
I simply pull my curtains back to look on paradise
again

by Fraser H, age 13.
Swanwick Lodge Secure Children's Home

Jack and Jill

Jack and Jill went up the hill
They were going up the hill because they had a deal
They had a race to the mill
Jack said to Jill, "If I win you should chill"
But when they raced, Jack fell down the hill
He was sent to hospital, he got given a pill
He got up but his mum said, "No you are ill"
She put him into bed because he looked very red
"I want to go out and play with Jill", he said
"This is the girl whom I want to wed"

by Jake P, age 15
Oakhill Secure Training centre

Falling through the cracks in the pavement

A stranger visiting my community
would see it with a stranger's eyes.

I live there and so
It seems normal and ordinary to me.
I see the things I expect to see,
See the things I expect to be there.

I see the bright lights, the shops, the crowds,
I hear the sound of voices, of music from other
cultures,
Savour the smells of food, of traffic and of
flowers.

The stranger would also see the street people,
the homeless, the gangs.
I see them too and I do know they are there,
but I don't notice them in the same way.

I live here, so that makes them a part of my
community,
But that is what they stay – a part, apart.

It isn't coming from another land that puts them
apart.
It isn't about race or religion.
It is about being the invisible people,
The people no-one seems to notice,
The people who have fallen through the cracks in
the pavement.

by Abbie A, age 15
Rainsbrook Secure Training Centre

Thinking about you

I think about you everyday and all the time
In my sleep I see you there
Wherever I go I see you
Even though we are so far apart
We seem so close
I always think about you day and night
I think about and just want to say
I love you
And hope that you are thinking about me too

by Oluwadamilare O, age 16
Oakhill Secure Training Centre

My Mind

In my life I want to be a good person
I wanna be somebody
Looked up to not falling down
I need to step up and stand my ground
Life is like a cup of tea to me
And that is not a joke.
I think of life with a little hope.
Doors slam, radios making stupid sounds
I want to go home me
Yeah I really do
I want to have fun
And do what teenagers do
Turn around and bang
That's bang in my face.
Now I've been smacked around
Wow that's a disgrace.
If I was on the out
That would be so unreal.
I would have made those biyches feel pain
That's bloody real,
Stop calling and shouting.
I don't want to know!
Gang life is my life
That's all you need to know!
I'm going to change now
The bad part of me is dead now
I look back and think
What was going through my head?

by Ananya M, age 16
Hassockfield Secure Training Centre

My Day Out

My name is Billy
And I'm very silly
I went to school
Fell in the pool
Went to the park
Saw a shark
Went back home
All alone

by Liam R, age 14
Swanwick Lodge Secure Children's Home

Breaking Free

Breaking free
Released from this place [Parc Prison]
Eternal life
Asking for forgiveness
Karing
L**i**ving
Nowhere to go
Going places
Freedom
Running thingz
Eternal freedom
Everlasting love

by Jordan T, age 16
HMP & YOI Parc

Freedom A Must

Prison oh prison
Oh what a rubbish place
Prosecution got me locked away
Parents phone once a day
Angry with my cell mates
Death to all my enemies
Oh God forgive me
My sins are cleared.

by Tito E, age 15
Medway Secure Training Centre

Being in custody is a waste of time
Cos when you get out you do more crime
Makes you think about things you've done
But sitting in here is no fun

The water gives you nasty spots
Makes you look like a dot to dot
Mattresses are full of fleas
Bites on arms and bites on knees

I'd be getting smashed on the out
From morning to night there's no doubt
Vodka and black would be great
I guess that I'll just have to wait

by Laura McW, age 15
Hassockfield Secure Training Centre

People

People, people, noise and keys,
Rattling, as staff walk by.
In a cell where time passes,
Slowly, and you can't run freely,
Over the green.
Never again.

by Courtney H, age 15
Medway Secure Training Centre

The Culture of football…..
Fernando Torres

It is really just a sport, a positive recreation
Or is it a new way of life, spread across the nation
People from the west, people from the east
A tool to use for governments to spread the word
of peace
World cups, Champions league, tournaments of
joy
Played in streets, played in parks by every g' land
boy
Dreams of lifting trophies, of being a superstar
A passion felt by plenty, by people near and far
His armband proved he was red, Torres, Torres
You'll never walk alone it said, Torres, Torres
We brought the boy from sunny spain
He gets the ball and scores again
Fernando Torres- Liverpool's number 9….

by Adam K, age 15
Oakhill Secure Training Centre

Voices: 3 connected haiku

Clamour of voices:
Accents, dialects: patois.
Amazing English

Medley or jumble?
A firework display of speech.
A gallimaufry.

Out of confusion
Comes meaning, understanding
Commonality.

by Aaron B, age 16
Rainsbrook Secure Training Centre

'I haven't seen the stars for ages'

by Jordan T, age 16
HMP & YOI Parc

If these walls were made of foam
I'd kick them down and fuck off home

If these walls were made of weed
I'd smoke it all 'til I was freed.

But since these walls are made of brick
I'll chill right here and do my rip.

by Kelly S, age 16
Hassockfield Secure Training Centre

Like

I like:
Playing basketball and volleyball
Listen to hip hop and techno
Painting graffiti
Play on PS3 and computers
Eat spaghetti and pizza, potatoes
Watch TV and good comedy, horrors and action film
I like to drive a car
I like Swanwick Lodge and I love Bad Girls

by Maciek C, age 15
Swanwick Lodge Secure Children's Home

Need 2 Change

I'm locked behind bars
Got nowhere to go
So I can't wait 'til I'm back on track
Time to roll
And stop digging myself in a deep hole
I need to keep my mind straight and get a job
Instead or lookin 4 manz to rob
Cos I'm so stressed
Sometimes I lay in my cell
So I can't just rest
And forget about things
I clear my mind of my dreams
Like a fat house a fine girl
Chains and diamond rings
'Cos the only thing I possess
Is a heart full of pain
So I need to get away see a better day
Instead of smoking weed
And drinking henny
Till I sway
And hit my pillow
Cos instead I
Feel hollow
And I feel the same tomorrow
So the light I need to follow

by Jacob S, age 17
HMP & YOI Parc

Peckham

People cry,
people die,
dat's the reason why
I want to stick to
Education,
to have a good College
for the key to my future,
I hope
Allah forgive me for my mistake.
I want to get a tattoo
Dat say R.I.P.
Mum

by Bedel Z, age 15
Medway Secure Training Centre

The cage around my cell window starts to shake,
As the wind blows and the sun begins to wake.
The light beams through, piercing my sleepy eyes,
Woken up everyday by the intensity of the sunrise.

The building echoes with laughter and some cries,
How you long for some fast food, burger, milkshake and fries.
Then your imaginings are disturbed by "Wakey, Wakey lads!"
Officers ordering us out of bed as if they were our dads.
You can try and ignore, shut your eyes and put the quilt over your head,
But getting up when told was inevitable if you wish to get fed.

The sound of the taps flowing is enough to send you barmy,
You see in jail you have a routine similar to that of the army.
Wake up when told, wash and brush as breakfast is soon.
Plastic bowls at the ready and don't forget your spoon.

Orders being dished out, until lock down at noon.
Dinner, then bang up, way before the presence of the moon.
Boredom is the key to deter you from this place.
If you have no T.V. then all there is to do is stare into space.

Frustration and loneliness are the images painted on your face.
Unless family isn't important and in that case,
These people enjoy the environment and adhere to the conditions,
But to most who miss home, being free is one of the main missions.
All in all you get fed well, socialise and exercise all the time,
But being free with family and friends is the key.
So forget about crime!

by Conor McP, age 16
HMYOI Stoke Heath

Medway is very
Easy, and the
Days go by quickly
Wished away
All the day you will think you come
Yesterday

by Ashley P, age 15
Medway Secure Training Centre

The frog prince

This tale began so long ago
About a frog prince, don't you know...
He needed the kiss of a pretty maid
To undo the curse the witch had made
The frog thought the situation was the worse
Until he remembered he could lift the curse
Sat on a log, by the local lake
The frog decided to wait and wait
He knew one day his princess would come
He was so bored sitting around on his bum
Then his luck suddenly changed
When his beautiful princess finally came

by Ricky T, age 16
Oakhill Secure Training Centre

Yo when you look at me
Tell me
What do you see?

You see a criminal but that's not me
Looking back on my life
Of criminality.

I didn't give a damn
But that's not who I am
You see it's not easy to change
Pick up my life and rearrange.

You need to slow down
Turn your head round
You're moving too fast.

I was walking down the street
I looked behind and there was the police
So I started thinking back to my past
History of criminality
And now you see
I'm in here for a very long time
For a little petty crime.

by Jason A, age 14
Hassockfield Secure Training Centre

Jimmy

Hello, my name is Jimmy
I know I can be a bit silly
I once went to bed and banged my head
And now I'm a bit dinny

And then I woke up

There once was a young boy

Hello, my name is Jimmy
I live in Swanwick Lodge
The food is a load of stodge
I go to bed at nine
But that does not pass the time

Then I wake up and go to school
And then I come back and jump in the pool
Hop back out and have a game of football
But that's what I do every day
I know it sounds a bit gay
But you should try it out
You are bound to like it without a doubt

by Jimmy A, age 14
Swanwick Lodge Secure Children's Home

Cocaine

Listen mate, if you think it's funny,
Crack Cocaine costs more than money.
If you've never had a pipe,
Let me tell you what it's like.
The very first one is very nice,
You'll never get that feeling twice.
Then you're out grafting day and night
Just to get your piece of white.
Then you come up in front of the Crown
And the fucking judge says "Send him down!"
And one thing's for sure for you and me,
We'll both end up in HMP.

by Rhys C, age 17
HMP & YOI Parc

72

Fantastic Mr Fox

Once upon a time there was a fox
Wearing red and yellow coloured socks
The fox was a dad of three
He was blind in one eye, so could hardly see

Bounce, Bodges and Bean
These are the farmers and they are mean
They owned chickens, geese and a fat juicy duck
Mr Fox was stealing these, but little did he know
he was pushing his luck

One night he said to his wife
'My darling, my love of my life
What shall it be tonight?'
For little did he know, he was going to have a
fright
Bean, Bodges and bounce
Were all ready to pounce

Guns were drawn

by Hayden O, age 15
Oakhill Secure Training Centre

Jack and the beanstalk

Jack and his mum had a row
She kicked him out and said, " Go sell this cow"
He wanted to sell the cow for trendy jeans
But traded them instead for magic beans
When he arrived back home
His mum was on the telephone
When he showed her what he had
She beat her boy very bad
He complained that she was very hard
She in turn called him a "retard"
She threw his beans out the door
And cried, "Our family is still poor"

But the beans grew very tall
Right over the garden wall
In the morning when he awoke
Climbing this plant would be a laugh and a joke
Up he climbed very high
And disappeared into the sky
He met a bird up at the top
She made him gasp and made him stop
She was a real beauty queen
The buffest girl he'd ever seen

But she belonged to giant that was scary
He was smelly, ugly and hairy
Jack asked the girl to leave the tower
She said she couldn't, she was under the giant's
power
Jack asked the giant to turn himself into a wild cat
To show his powers by turning himself in to a rat
Jack pretended to play games
But then threw the rat in to the flames
The beautiful girl was happy as larry
And promised Jack that she would marry

Jack's mum was worried while he was away
But when she saw his rich bride, she was happy
'til her dying day

by Dami O, age 16
Oakhill Secure Training Centre

21st Century!

Children these days care more for their
reputation,
Than going to school to get an education.
I wish I never entered the system,
But at the time it seemed fun.
Now I'm starting to change by
Doing crime not last,
Be like me look to future stop looking at the past.
You could walk down the street,
It could be a member of your family
Or a friend lay dead at your feet.
Racism, freckles or even the colour of your hair,
Children these days love to laugh and stare
Drink, drugs, knives and guns,
It could be one of your daughters or sons.
Put your commitment in to stop it,
Because at the moment people are helping feed
it.
How much we seem to screem and yelp,
No-one never wants to seem to HELP!

by Nardein M, age 15
Medway Secure Training Centre

Sad

You say you care but you don't
You say you are here to help but you don't
You say you will always be there but you are not
The day you left me I was mad
But now I'm just sad

by Kirsten W, age 16
Swanwick Lodge Secure Children's Home

Prison boy wrote home one day
Found his true loves gone away
When he asked the reason why
She answered him with this reply
If you choose the honest life
Surely I will be your wife
If you choose the life of crime
Prison boy do your time
Late that night in his cell
Prison boy rang his bell
Screws came running to his door
Prison boy was on his floor
In his hand a note all red
In his hand a note that said
Dig it wide and dig it deep
Plant red roses at my feet
On my chest a turtle dove
Tell the world I died for love

by Daniel B, age 18
HMP & YOI Wetherby

I am the black kid
A poem exploring identity

I am a black kid who got locked up
I am a black kid who girls think is hot
I am a black kid who never ran from beef
I am a black kid who had friends on every street
I am a black kid who a lot of kids hate
I am a black kid who loves to eat cake
I am a black kid who made my mum sad
I am a black kid who wants to make my mum glad
I am a black kid who done some bad things
I am a black kid who never likes to sing
I am a black kid who had a bad life
I am a black kid who wants to put things right
I am a black kid who hates the police
Yes I am a black kid and I did lock down half the street.

by Tafari C, age 14
Oakhill Secure Training Centre

The Key

I've tried to walk away but I keep coming back
I've tried to move on but I just can't
I guess it's time I face the truth....I just can't get
over you
When I tell you I love you
I don't say it out of habit
Or to make conversation
I say it to remind you that you're the best thing
that ever happened to me

She says she doesn't care
But the look in her eyes tells a completely
different story
They may be confused about a lot of things
But she knows the only time she's truly happy is
when she is with him....

I'll love you till the day I die coz that makes the
time go by
He is the only one that has the key
And the only one that can smash it up into three
And I love this boy
So leave us be.....

by Sammiiz B, age 16
Swanwick Lodge Secure Children's Home

My Mind

I feel as tho
My mind has run low
The hurt I possess
Has caused
So much stress
People may say
I'm a thug
But not true
Who do you trust
Me aw them
Up to you
If I had the chance to sho them
Wot I've shown you
Maybe then they'd believe
I'm a human being 2

by Adam M, age 17
HMP & YOI Parc

Stuck in a place called Hassockfield
No cigs, no booze, no drugs.
Wanna go out and see my family
But stupid me has been an angry kid.

Plenty of doors but they all get locked
I'd be out if I could get some keys
I wish I didn't commit the crime
Then I wouldn't be doin my time.

No family, no friends, no nothing
Here lonely all alone
But time's quick. I'm nearly out
Two weeks and I'll be home.

Committing crime gives you a thrill
But bein locked up's not fun
Missing summer, ice cream and friends
Never seeing the sun.

Committing crime may give you a buzz
Cars flying past with blue lights flashing
But, back in court, same old face
Sooner or later you'll be doin your time.

When I get out you'll see me change
Being a criminal ain't good

Plenty of doors and they all get locked
No family, no friends, no nothing

Where would you rather be?

by Keeley W, age 17
Hassockfield Secure Training Centre

Being locked up I can't fish
Can't see the sun on the water,
Feel the wind on my face,
Watch the wild life in the fields.
Feel the sun on my face, and then,
The line goes tight.
I'm in for a fight with this fish.
Just the fish and me.
If he's a trout,
I'll eat him for tea.

by Tom C, age 15
Medway Secure Training Centre

Jack and the Beanstalk

Jack and his mum are very poor
His mum said, 'Go on, get out the door
Take this lazy cow,
And sell it any how
He got no cash because he was not keen
So he swapped it for some beans
When he returned empty handed to his home
His mum hit him around his head with a phone
'You should of brought home something more,
Throw those lousy beans out the door.
Get to bed straight away, you clown
No supper for you and don't come down!'

In the night the beans grew and grew
It went up into the sky so blue
He decided to climb the stalk
Dreaming that at the top, would be roast pork
At the top he found a chest
He grabbed the gold and shoved it under his vest
The giant was trying to hunt Jack down
He shouted, "I'm going to break your neck, you clown"

Jack was slippy, slick and quick
He had to pull out a trick
In his back pocket there was a tin of pepper spray
He aimed it at the giant's face and blasted away
The vicious giant
Began to cry
Tripped over the stalk and fell out the sky

When Jack got home, he showed his mum the
money
His mum was happy– "Oh Jack, you're my
homey!"

by Reece R, age 16
Oakhill Secure Training Centre

Can't sleep at night,
Moving left and right,
Away from my family,
Overnight,
Yet my hopes are up and down,
One day Mother you will be mine,
Day and night,
Whatever the weather,
We will be together.

by Akmol M, age 13
Medway Secure Training Centre

Registered Charity No. 1041855

Youth at Risk is honoured to receive the proceeds of this book. We are a groundbreaking charity dedicated to making a positive and lasting change to the lives of vulnerable young people who, lacking self-esteem, aspiration and motivation, see their futures as pre-destined to be ones of hopelessness, unemployment and even crime.

They need and deserve support to enable them to change their mind-sets and remove the barriers that are obstructing them – to form a more positive view of themselves, to recognize that they have potential and value, to realize that they do have options and choices, to empower them to take control of their lives and responsibility for their actions.

Youth at Risk has been designing and delivering training and coaching programmes for these young people and the professionals that support them for over 16 years.

We can't write poetry – but we can wax lyrical about our track record, which is one of being highly innovative, of enabling change to occur and of making a powerful impact on young people's lives.

Neil Wragg MBE
Chief Executive
www.youthatrisk.org.uk